1

2

3

6

The Good and the Bad Trees.

Luke 6 : 43 - 45.

By

John C Burt.

8

10

1.

FOREWORD :

This is a book that deals with an image of the good and bad trees and their fruit from the very words of the Lord Jesus Christ in Luke 6 : 43 - 45. This image of good and bad trees was an image that was rather a common one for the Lord Jesus Christ to use . The image of Luke 6 : 43 - 45 has parallels in Matthew 7 : 15 - 20 and in John 15 : 1 - 8, where the image is taken much further by the Lord Jesus Christ and has reference to the vine.

I for one love the image of good and bad trees and their fruit because it helps me to think about people and how they present and what the fruit of their lives really is? As you would understand sometimes we can have people in our own lives who produce

good fruit in our lives and
other times we can have
people in our lives who
produce bad fruit. Also, at
times we can be people who
in and of themselves either
produce good or bad fruit.

The words of the
Lord Jesus Christ in the Gospel
of Luke are an echo of some
sort of the contents of the
Wisdom Literature of the
Word of God. I am thinking
particularly of the Proverbs
and the Psalter itself, both

which are very similar to the images of the good and bad trees and their fruit in the New Testament. One could also think of Psalm one, the tree planted by the water that provides good fruit and prospers. Whereas, the wicked tree or the bad tree produces bad fruit in their lives.

John 15 : 1 - 8, takes the image of the good and bad trees and their fruit. Which in some ways, reflects the reality of the Gospel of John being a highly developed theological thought within it's Gospel. The good and bad trees and their fruit are used to further the concept and need for disciple's to abide in the Lord Jesus Christ. The Lord Jesus Christ states within these verses very clearly that apart from abiding in Him, a disciple can do nothing. All which takes and develops the image of the good and bad trees and their fruit to a much greater level of thought and importance as well.

18

2.

Once again, as we seek to discuss and give consideration to the image of good and bad trees will consider four different versions of each text from the Word of God.

(CEB)

Matthew 7 : 15 - 20.

(15) " Watch out for false prophets. They come to you dressed like sheep, but inside they are vicious wolves.

(16) You will know them by their fruit. Do people get bunches of grapes from thorny weeds, or do they get figs from thistles?

(17) In the same way, every good tree produces good fruit, and every rotten tree produces bad fruit.

(18) A good tree can't produce bad fruit. And a rotten tree can't produce good fruit.

(19) Every tree that doesn't produce good fruit is chopped down and thrown into the fire.

(20) Therefore, you will know them by their fruit."

Luke 6 : 43 - 45.

(43) " A good tree doesn't produce bad fruit, nor does a bad tree produce good fruit.

(44) Each tree is known by its own fruit. People do not gather figs from thorny plants, nor do they pick grapes from prickly bushes.

22

(45) A good person produces good from the good treasury of the inner self, while an evil person produces evil from the evil treasury of the inner self. The inner self overflows with words that are spoken."

John 15 : 1 - 8.

(1) " I am the true vine , and my Father is the vineyard keeper.

(2) He removes any of my branches that don't produce fruit, and he trims any branch that produces fruit so that it will produce even more fruit.

(3) You are already trimmed because of the word I have spoken to you.

(4) Remain in me, and I will remain in you. A branch can't produce fruit by itself, but you must remain in the vine.

Likewise, you can't produce fruit unless you remain in me.

(5) I am the vine; you are the branches. If you remain in me and I in you, then you will produce much fruit. Without me, you can't do anything.

(6) If you don't remain in me, you will be like a branch that is thrown out and dries up. Those branches are gathered up, and thrown into a fire, and burned.

(7) If you remain in me and my words remain in you, ask for whatever yo want and it will be done for you.

(8) My Father is glorified when you produce much fruit and in this way prove that you are my disciples."

(NIV)

Matthew 7 : 15 - 20.

(15) " Watch out for false prophets. They come to you in sheep's clothing but inwardly they are ferocious wolves.

(16) By their fruit you will recognize them. Do people pick grapes from thornbushes, or figs from thistles?

(17) Likewise every good tree bears good fruit, but a bad tree bears bad fruit.

(18) A good tree cannot bear bad fruit, and a bad tree cannot bear good fruit.

(19) Every tree that does not bear good fruit is cut down and thrown into the fire.

(20) Thus, by their fruit you will recognize them."

Luke 6 : 43 - 45.

(43) " No good tree bears

bad fruit, nor does a bad tree bear good fruit.

(44) Each tree is recognized by its own fruit. People do not pick figs from thornbushes, or grapes from briers.

(45) The good man brings good things out of the good stored up in his heart, and the evil man brings evil things out of the evil stored up in his heart. For out of the overflow of his heart his mouth speaks."

John 15 : 1 - 8.

(1) " I am the true vine, and my Father is the gardener.

(2) He cuts off every branch in me that bears no fruit, while every branch that does bear fruit he prunes so that it will be even more fruitful.

(3) You are already clean because of the word I have spoken to you.

(4) Remain in me, and I will remain in you. No branch can bear fruit by itself; it must remain in the vine. Neither can you bear fruit unless you remain in me.

(5) " I am the vine; you are the branches . If a man remains in me and I in him, he will bear much fruit; apart from me you can do nothing.

(6) If anyone does not remain in me, he is like a branch that is thrown away

and withers; such branches
are picked up, thrown into
the fire and burned.

(7) If you remain in me
and my words remain in you,
ask whatever you wish, and
it will be given you.

(8) This is my Father's
glory, that you bear much
fruit, showing yourselves to
be my disciples. "

(GNT)

Matthew 7 : 15 - 20.

(15) " Be on your guard against false prophets; they come to you looking like sheep on the outside, but on the inside they are really like wild wolves.

(16) You will know them by what they do. Thorn bushes do not bear grapes, and briers do not bear figs.

(17) A healthy tree bears good fruit, but a poor tree bears bad fruit.

(18) A healthy tree cannot bear bad fruit, and a poor tree cannot bear good fruit.

(19) And any tree that does not bear good fruit is cut down and thrown in the fire.

(20) So then, you will

know the false prophets by what they do."

Luke 6 : 43 - 45.

(43) " A healthy tree does not bear bad fruit, nor does a poor tree bear good fruit.

(44) Every tree is known by the fruit it bears, you do not pick figs from thorn bushes or gather grapes from bramble bushes.

(45) A good person brings good out of the treasure of good things in his heart; a bad person brings bad out of his treasure of bad things. For the mouth speaks what the heart is full of."

John 15 : 1 - 8.

(1) " I am the real vine, and my Father is the gardener.

(2) He breaks off every branch in me that does not bear fruit, and he prunes every

branch that does bear fruit, so that it will be clean and bear more fruit.

(3) You have been made clean already by the teaching I have given you.

(4) Remain united to me, and I will remain united to you. A branch cannot bear fruit by itself; it can do so only if it remains in the vine. In the same way you cannot bear fruit unless you remain in me.

(5) " I am the vine, and you are the branches. Those who remain in me, and I in them, will bear much fruit; for you can do nothing without me.

(6) Those who do not remain in me are thrown out like a branch and dry up; such branches are gathered up and thrown into the fire, where they are burned.

(7) If you remain in me

and my words remain in you,
then you will ask for
anything you wish, and you
shall have it.

(8) My Father's glory is
shown by your bearing much
fruit; and in this way you
become my disciples."

(ESV)

Matthew 7 : 15 - 20.

(15) " Beware of false prophets, who come to you in sheep's clothing but inwardly are ravenous wolves.

(16) You will recognize them by their fruits. Are grapes gathered from thornbushes, or figs from thistles?

(17) So, every healthy tree bears good fruit, but the diseased tree bears bad fruit.

(18) A healthy tree cannot bear bad fruit, nor can a diseased tree bear good fruit.

(19) Every tree that does not bear good fruit is cut down and thrown into the fire.

(20) Thus you will recognize them by their fruits. "

Luke 6 : 43 - 45.

(43) " For no good tree bears bad fruit, nor again does a bad tree bear good fruit,

(44) for each tree is known by its own fruit, For figs are not gathered from thornbushes, nor are grapes picked from a bramble bush.

(45) The good person out of the good treasure of his

heart produces good, and the evil person out of his evil treasure produces evil, for out of the abundance of the heart his mouth speaks."

John 15 : 1 - 8.

(1) " I am the true vine, and my father is the vindresser.

(2) Every branch in me that does not bear fruit he takes away, and every

branch that does bear fruit he prunes, that it may bear more fruit.

(3) Already you are clean because of the word that I have spoken to you.

(4) Abide in me, and I in you. As the branch cannot bear fruit by itself, unless it abides in the vine, neither can you, unless you abide in me.

(5) I am the vine; you are the branches. Whoever abides in

me and I in him, he it is that bears much fruit, for apart from me you can do nothing.

(6) If anyone does not abide in me he is thrown away like a branch and withers; and the branches are gathered, thrown into the fire, and burned.

(7) If you abide in me, and my words abide in you, ask whatever you wish, and it will be done for you.

(8) By this my Father is glorified, that you bear much fruit and so prove to be my disciples."

50

3.

What we are going to do in this chapter is to consider the Scriptural Citation from Matthew 7 : 15 - 20. I will give you at least two different versions of the text.

Matthew 7 : 15 - 20.

(CEB)

(15) " Watch out for false prophets . They come to you dressed like sheep, but inside they are vicious wolves.

(16) You will know them by their fruit. Do people get bunches of grapes from thorny weeds, or do they get figs from thistles?

(17) In the same way, every good tree produces good fruit, and every rotten tree produces bad fruit.

(18) A good tree can't produce bad fruit. And a rotten tree can't produce good fruit.

(19) Every tree that doesn't produce good fruit is chopped down and thrown into the fire.

(20) Therefore, you will know them by their fruit."

Matthew 7 : 15 - 20.

(NIV)

(15) " Watch out for false prophets. They come to you in sheep's clothing, but inwardly they are ferocious wolves.

(16) By their fruit you

will recognize them. Do people pick grapes from thornbushes, or figs from thistles?

(17) Likewise every good tree bears good fruit, but a bad tree bears bad fruit.

(18) A good tree cannot bear bad fruit, and a bad tree cannot bear good fruit.

(19) Every tree that does not bear good fruit is cut

down and thrown into the fire.

(20) Thus, by their fruit you will recognize them."

The message of Matthew 7 : 15 - 20 is largely concerned with good and bad trees and their fruit. It opens with a call to watch out for false prophets and then goes onto discuss in detail the good and bad trees and their fruit.

One could naturally assume that the reference to good and bad trees and their fruit is solely concerned with the false prophets and yet I do not believe this to be the case. I believe the image of the good and bad trees and their fruit has far wider application to all people's. In some ways the immediate referent point is the false prophet's but I would believe that the Lord Jesus Christ has a far wider audience and population in His mind?

I love the imagery of good and bad trees and their fruit because it is in itself a very earthy agricultural image; it very down - to - earth. People would have been able to relate to the very imagery of the good and bad trees that the Lord Jesus Christ was using.

In the end, it's significant that a good tree cannot produce bad fruit and a bad tree cannot produce good fruit. The thing, is to be a good tree and then you are guaranteed of producing and showing and revealing through your very life good fruit. The good tree can only produce the good fruit it does because it is rooted and founded and sustained in and by the Lord Jesus Christ. To take the imagery further and to it's ultimate conclusion. Conversely , the bad tree produces bad fruit because it is not rooted and founded and sustained by the Lord Jesus Christ?

The imagery of the good and bad trees and their respective fruit holds true if one sits back for a time and considers the world we all live in and the various sorts and types of individual's that go to make it up. I would simply say, that I am sure we would all know people we would say are good trees and also that we would people we would say are bad trees. At times the thing can be that we tend to do avoid the people who are bad trees and default to the people who are good trees in our lives and through them.

Matthew 7 : 15 - 20 states that you can know a person by the very fruit that their lives produce and exhibit within them. I think that's always the check on our interactions with the various people and individual's in our own lives. Someone once said to me an apple tree does not have to think too much about producing apples , it just does. This is also, largely true of good people , they do not have to think too much about producing good fruit in their own lives, it just sort of happens .... There is so such thing as sweating and grinding your teeth to produce an apple and in our case good fruit, it sort of just follows that it will happen. In particular for those people who heart's are good, the good fruit comes out of their very being , it's produced by the overflow of their own heart's.

The Lord Jesus Christ graphically demonstrates all of this for us in the verses of Matthew 7 : 15 - 20. Put simply in terms of His imagery, if you want good fruit you do not go seeking it from trees that in and of themselves cannot hope to produce the good fruit you are seeking. Think grapes from thornbushes and you are there. Or even more blatantly, figs from thistles?

4.

What we are going to do in this chapter is to consider Luke 6 : 43 - 45 and seek to discuss the implications of it , in relation to our ongoing discussion of good and bad trees.

Luke 6 : 43 - 45.

(ESV)

(43) " For no good tree bears bad fruit, nor again does a bad tree bear good fruit,

(44) for each tree is known by its own fruit. For figs are not gathered from thornbushes, nor are grapes picked from a bramble bush.

(45) The good person out of the good treasure of his heart produces good, and the evil person out of his evil treasure produces evil, for out of the abundance of the heart his mouth speaks."

Luke 6 : 43 - 45.

(GNT)

(43) " A healthy tree does not bear bad fruit, nor does a poor tree bear good fruit.

(44) Every tree is known by the fruit it bears; you do not pick figs from thorn bushes or gather grapes from bramble bushes.

(45) A good person brings good out of the treasure of good things in his heart; a bad person brings bad out of his treasure of bad things. For

the mouth speaks what the heart is full of ."

Luke 6 : 43 - 45 takes the imagery surrounding the good and bad trees to a higher level and really highlights the reality that it is by their fruit that you can know a person. Just as tree is known by the fruit that it produces , so to is a person known by the very fruit that their life produces. Good trees produce good fruit and conversely bad trees produce bad fruit.

The verses from the Gospel of Luke , take the concept and notion of the good and bad trees much further and really highlights the reality that it is by their fruit that you can know a person. It is out of the treasury of a good heart that the good person will produce good fruit and vice versa with a bad person and bad fruit. The idea of people having a treasury of good or bad , or evil within them, is one that is interesting and at the same time a profound thought as well. Therefore, the fruit that a person produces comes in reality from within their own particular treasury of good, bad or evil actions and intentions from within their own heart's.

Again, I would hazard a guess and believe that the person can only produce the very things that a relationship with the Lord Jesus Christ and ongoing fellowship with Him has put in their lives and heart's.

The particular fruit of a person's life is determined by their relationship, fellowship and the ongoing work of the Holy Spirit and the Lord Jesus Christ in their very lives. One cannot just think about producing fruit that is fact good from within themselves, it has to be within the person, brought about by the Lord Jesus Christ and the Holy Spirit working in and through their lives. In some ways , in our day and age , this might seem to be very much a moot point and yet I believe it is worth stating very clearly. Because in our days and our age, there is much development and help on being the better self, the wholesome person and self - image and personal growth. In the face of all this , one could think and come to the belief , that you just have to think very hard , and generate the good fruit from somewhere inside of yourself? These very verses from the Gospel of Luke, put an end to such thinking, believing and postulating on our part.

5.

Consideration will now
be given to the verses from
John 15 : 1 - 8. These verses
will be discussed in terms
of our overall theme of
good and bad trees.

John 15 : 1 - 8.

(NIV)

(1) " I am the true vine, and my Father is the gardener.

(2) He cuts off every branch in me that bears no fruit, while every branch that does bear fruit he prunes so that it will be even more fruitful .

(3) You are already clean because of the word I have spoken to you.

(4) Remain in me, and I will remain in you. No branch can bear fruit by itself; it must remain in the vine. Neither can you bear fruit unless you remain in me.

(5) " I am the vine; you are the branches. If a man remains in me and I in him, he will bear much fruit; apart

from me you can do nothing.

(6) If anyone does not remain in me, he is like a branch that is thrown away and withers; such branches are picked up, thrown into the fire and burned.

(7) If you remain in me and my words remain in you, ask whatever you wish, and it will be given you.

(8) This is to my father's glory, that you bear much fruit, showing yourselves to be my disciples."

John 15 : 1 - 8.

(CEB)

(1) " I am the true vine, and my father is the vineyard keeper.

(2) He removes any

of my branches that don't produce fruit, and he trims any branch that produces fruit so that it will produce even more fruit.

(3) You are already trimmed because of the word I have spoken to you.

(4) Remain in me, and I will remain in you. A branch can't produce fruit by itself, but must remain in the vine. Likewise, you can't

produce fruit unless you remain in me.

(5) I am the vine; you are the branches. If you remain in me and I in you, then you will produce much fruit. Without me, you can't do anything.

(6) If you don't remain in me, you will be like a branch that is thrown out and dries up. Those branches are gathered up, thrown into a fire, and burned.

(7) If you remain in me and my words remain in you, ask for whatever you want and it will be done for you.

(8) My Father is glorified when you produce much fruit and in this way prove that you are my disciples."

In the end, I simply believe that what we have in

the Gospel of John, is a continuation of the theme of good and bad trees from the other Gospel accounts. The image , is I must admit different in so many ways and yet it still has a focus on fruit of the vine, think the fruit of the good and bad trees from the earlier verses considered by this book. This time , the Lord Jesus Christ, is the tree or the vine that the branches are in reality attached to. The branches of the vine , receive their life and sustenance from abiding in

the vine, which is of course by
abiding and remaining in the
Lord Jesus Christ Himself.

The verses in the
Gospel of John , take the
imagery of good and bad
trees and their fruit and
develop it much further
theologically, in theological
thought, concepts and
notions. The constant refrain
of these verses from John's
Gospel, is that, to put it
simply, unless one abides and
remains joined to and
attached to the the true vine,

then one has no hope or even ability to produce the good fruit. In our days and our generations, the word abiding in the Lord Jesus Christ and remaining in Him , has largely lost it's meaning and even it's importance to everyday Christians in the Christian Church. Yet, many of th Saints of old, those who are dotted throughout the long and varied history of the Christian Church, they knew what it was to abide and even remain in the true vine, which is of course to abide and remain in the Lord Jesus Christ. It may well be something of the Christian Faith, that we all need to rediscover and seek to put into practice in and through our own lives.

The difference with this imagery of the vine, and the true vine of the Lord Jesus Christ, is that, there is a sting in the tail and the branches that do not bear fruit, good fruit and thrown away and burned up. So, in this imagery of the vine and bearing good fruit, there are inherent consequences inbuilt to it all. To not be someone who in reality produces good fruit in an ongoing manner and is in reality a bad tree, then that branch or tree is faced with the consequences of being thrown out and being destroyed by fire. In many ways, this all takes the concept of good and bad trees and the very need to be trees that produce good fruit to it's logical conclusion and end result in the Lord Jesus

Christ.

In conclusion, it is interesting to note, that through the true disciples and true trees and true branches of the Lord Jesus Christ producing good fruit, the Father is glorified. All of which, is more reasons to be good trees and true branches of the true vine who produce good fruit. Simply, because in doing this simple thing, we prove to be the true disciple of the Lord Jesus Christ and bring glory to both the Father and the name of the Son of God , Jesus Christ.

The other thing, to note from verse eight, is that, there will not only some fruit produced by those who are true branches of the vine and good trees but rather much fruit , an abundance of good fruit. For those who are true branches of the vine, good trees they will in reality produce much fruit, that will last and it all comes from abiding and remaining in the true vine, the Lord Jesus Christ.

6.

EPILOGUE :

This book has sought to discuss the concept of good and bad trees and their fruit, as presented in the New Testament of the Word of God. In the end it is all about the fruit that is produced by one's life. We saw how a bad tree cannot produce good fruit whereas a good tree can only produce good fruit.

This was an agricultural image and imagery used by the Lord Jesus Christ to make and illustrate his points about the need for people to be good trees and therefore produce good fruit. We also saw, how this image and imagery comes out of the Wisdom Literature of the Word of God, the Book of Proverbs and the Psalter itself.

One only has to think of Psalm one to see this conclusion holds true of the Psalter and Wisdom Literature in general.

Also, it was seem how the verses from the Gospel of John develop and elaborate upon the image and imagery of good and bad trees of the other Gospels. This is partly due to the very reality that the Gospel of John , is definitely a more theologically developed Gospel than either Matthew or Luke's Gospel's.

A fitting conclusion to this book and our consideration and discussion of both good and bad trees and their fruit, is that, by bearing good fruit we glorify the Father the LORD GOD ALMIGHTY. We also, through the very bearing of fruit that is good and lots of it , that we are in reality disciple's of the Lord Jesus Christ, who are in reality true disciple's of Him.

Finally, we bear

good fruit and fruit that will last by both abiding and remaining in the Lord Jesus Christ. He is very clear , apart from abiding and remaining in Himself we cannot do anything by ourselves, in relation to bearing good fruit and fruit that will last and also glorify the Father the LORD GOD ALMIGHTY.

THE AUTHOR :

JOHN C BURT .

John worships at St. Phillip's , Anglican Church, Auburn , NSW , Australia .

John loves coffee and enjoys the odd cup of coffee in the cafes of Auburn.

John also loves Chinese food as well as Indian food. He also, enjoys the odd Pizza , any sort of Pizza ...

AMEN AND AMEN AND AMEN.

SHALOM ....

Lightning Source UK Ltd.
Milton Keynes UK
UKHW020633081019
351160UK00001B/7/P